Believe in Yourself, Girl

Other titles by Ashley Rice
Published by
Blue Mountain Arts®

Girls Rule
You Are a Girl Who Can Do Anything
You Are a Girl Who Totally Rocks!

Library of Congress Control Number: 2021938105
ISBN: 978-1-68088-388-6

Blue Mountain Press is registered in U.S. Patent and Trademark Office.

Certain trademarks are used under license.

Printed in China.
First Printing: 2021

Blue Mountain Arts, Inc.
P.O. Box 4549, Boulder, Colorado 80306

...a very special book
for a girl who
is meant for
great things

Ashley Rice

Blue Mountain Press™
Boulder, Colorado

Believe in Yourself, Girl

Believe in yourself
and all you want to be.
Don't let what
other people say
or do make you frown.
Laugh as much as possible.
Let in the good times
and get through the bad.
Be happy with who
and where you are.
You are in the right place,
and your heart is leading you
on the way to a great tomorrow.

When circumstances
seem difficult,
pull through them.
This will make you
stronger than you think.
The longer you practice
the habit of working
toward your dreams,
the easier the journey
will become.
You are meant for great things.
Learn as much as possible.
Always follow your dreams.

You Can Achieve Anything in This World

Every day, remind yourself of all the things you are good at and all that you are capable of accomplishing in every area of your life. You are amazing in every way, and you should always remember that! Don't let other people discourage you from reaching for your dreams. What you do is up to you, because you are the only one who knows what you are capable of.

Envision yourself succeeding. Imagine what you are going to accomplish, and then take the steps to actually achieve what you want to do. Keep your eyes on the prize at all times, and don't let any missteps discourage you in any way. Focus on the future and all you can do to make it unforgettable. You are irreplaceable and incredible. Great things are coming your way — all you have to do is believe in yourself... and go for it!

Just be yourself —
no matter what circumstances
you may face or what you might encounter
as you go through your days.
People will try to tell you who to be,
but don't listen to them!
Instead, go your own way.
Sing your own song.
Do what you know you
were born to do.
Opportunities will inevitably
come your way, and you've
got to recognize them
and be ready to take
advantage of them.
You can only do that
if you are your true,
authentic self at all times.

Nothing good ever came
from being "fake"
or just doing things to fit in
with the rest of the crowd.
The true trailblazers of this
life are the ones who
followed their own dreams,
regardless of what the rest
of the world was doing.
So trust in your heart
and your mind to lead the way,
and always be yourself...
because you are one of a kind,
and no one can ever
compete with that!

You Deserve the Best in Every Way

Don't you dare —
even for an instant —
think that you
don't deserve or "need"
all of the good things
coming your way!
You deserve the very best,
and you shouldn't be afraid
to ask for it
or accept it with open arms
when it's offered to you.

You've worked hard
and put in the time and effort
that was needed
to get the job done.
You should receive
the greatest rewards ever
in return for all your hard work.
So just know that
you are an amazing person
with many different gifts and talents
to offer the world.
You're brilliant and disciplined
and admired for all
the things you do
each and every day.

How to Stay True to Who You Are

- Never say anything you would not want repeated back to you.

- Walk away when angry. Return only if you truly need to.

- Expect little, but work like there is no tomorrow.

- Be independent of praise, push criticism aside, and recognize feedback.

- Count your blessings rather than your troubles.

- Leave grudges behind, confront obstacles you see whenever you can, and always carry courage with you.

- Know the world is never perfect (and that includes you). See the beauty in its flaws, while also striving to improve it... and you.

- If you can make someone's day, never fail to do so.

- Remember that you have the right to be you.

Don't Compare Yourself to Others

Accept and love yourself
for exactly who you are.
And don't compare
yourself to others —
there will always be someone
with a better this or a fancier that.
Plus, the people you're comparing
yourself to most likely
wish that they had some
of the outstanding personal
qualities that _you_ possess.

If you look around,
you will see that the people
who are the happiest
aren't the ones who have
the most stuff, but the
people who empower
themselves and believe
in who they are as individuals.
They recognize their own
strengths and strive to be
the best that they can be.
So don't waste any time worrying about
what you think you lack.
Be happy with who you are.

There Will Never Be Another You

There will never be
another you.
Go chase down your dreams —
make them come true.
Time flies like a bird...
and you?
You've got these great dreams,
these plans...
so see them through.

You live just once;
love what you do.
The world spins fast,
so make the good times last,
knowing this is true:
you've got big dreams,
you've got these plans...
and there will never be
another you.

Pop Quiz!

<u>You Are:</u>

A) Brave

B) Amazing

C) Unique

D) Irreplaceable

E) Inspiring

CORRECT ANSWER:

F) All of the above

EXTRA CREDIT ANSWER:

And so much more!

Remember...
You Can Make
a Difference

You can do things that matter.
You can make a difference.
You can come through
with a solid victory
whenever it's important
or even when it is minor.
And sometimes you can even
completely save the day.

You can make your way
through the world
with truth, humor, and love...
and that will make all the difference!

Be the Change You Need

Things you can't change:
- ● Your past
- ○ Your biological family
- ● Users and haters
- ● Other people's attitudes
- ○ What you did yesterday

Things you can change:

- ○ Your situation and/or environment
- ◕ Your perspective
- ◐ Your education levels
- ◑ Your health
- ○ Your self-esteem
- ◐ Your boundaries   ✓
- ◕ Your posture   ˅
- ◕ Your confidence
- ○ Today...
        and all your tomorrows

Stand Tall

Keep a true, real heart.
Grow by always facing life
with an open perspective.
If people do not see things
through your view, try not to
engage in the same arguments
with them over and over again —
just walk away
and do your own thing.
Make diligence and
persistence your friends.

You do not have to prove yourself
to anyone besides you.
To your heart, stay true.
And through it all:
Grin and face the days
with curiosity and wonder.
Find the rainbows in the rain,
the comet in the darkness...
and you will always shine.
Defend your strengths by
doing what you love to do...
and you will be amazing!

Follow Your You

There is no blueprint for a great life. Every person's mind and heart are different, and no two lives are the same. Try not to place any blame on the past — that will only slow you down. Do learn from it... then move beyond it. Even if you do not think you have all the right answers yet, know that sometimes the questions matter the most anyway.

As you progress step by step, you will grow
and know more about yourself and the
world each year.

All you've got to do is trust your heart,
     place some faith in the universe...
          and follow your you.

If You Have a Dream...

To make it true,
run through
the paces
in your mind.
Try hard,
then harder than
you once did before.
Don't wait too long to
give life your all,
and do your best
every day.
Always find a way.
Lend hope everything you've got.
When it comes to closed doors,
open them.
When it comes to giving up,
don't.

Believe you can —
and you will.

It is a risk to
greet each new day
with a dream in your heart.
It is a risk to speak.
It is a risk to take a chance
on trust, a worthy cause,
love, luck, or destiny.
It is a risk to open a door
and walk right on through.
It might be a risk to do anything!
But the question is...
can you live with
the disappointment
you will keep
inside your mind
if you decide not to?

Take a chance on friendship, fame,
charity, furthering knowledge,
human kindness, being brave...
being _you_.

Go for it!

LIFE!

When Preparing for Something You Want to Do...

Ask yourself these things:

1. How can I rock this?
2. How can I have a sense of humor if I mess something up?
3. How can I push myself beyond my past limits?
4. How can I rid myself of the fear that I am not good enough?
5. How can I be a winner, no matter what the outcome?

6. How can I move forward if I don't get the results I expect?
7. How can I find my inner hero?
8. How can I save my own day?

The answer to all these questions is...

By finding hope inside of me so that I can be more than I was yesterday again tomorrow... by refusing to stop believing in me!

To Chase After a Dream, What Do You Really Need?

A determined will
A mind that sometimes
   craves being free
A spirit that needs to be wild
   and at other times
   wants to be still
A pair of shoes tied to swift feet
   for moving forward
The ability to be patient
Wings for chasing stars

But mostly you need a belief in
yourself and a brave, true heart.
They will take you further than
all these things put together.

How to Succeed at Everything You Put Your Mind To

 Set high standards for yourself and don't be afraid to try to achieve them. If you set the bar high to begin with, you will reach what you're shooting for and maybe even far beyond that.

Hold on to each and every moment. Life goes by so fast and you don't want to miss a single second of it. You want to be able to look back and see a past filled with fond memories — whether you had a blast or learned something important that you can live by.

Do something you enjoy for at least a few minutes every day. What you choose to do today may open doors for you tomorrow.

Always speak your mind no matter who is present (as long as you aren't hurting anyone by doing so). Stand by what you say and say what you mean.

Embrace change. Face down your fears. Don't feel bad about the past. Hold on to only those memories that you want or most need to remember. Find hope in the everyday.

Choose to See Life Through a Positive Mindset

If you head into any situation
saying to yourself,
"I can do this! It will be great,"
99 percent of the time,
no matter what the outcome may be,
you will choose to see it as a success.

This is because when you have
a positive outlook on life,
everything you see
is framed within that view.
If you start to do something thinking,
"Everything I do is wrong, and I will mess up,"
99 percent of the time, whatever the details,
you will interpret your results as a failure.
The exterior circumstances of a person's life
are not what determine
whether they can be happy.
Happiness is always an option...
if you just choose it.

Don't Be Too
Hard on Yourself

There's a big difference
between self-reflection
and criticism.
The first helps you
see things as they are
and learn from them
and deal with them.
The second is just you
putting yourself down for
no good reason...
and there is never
a good enough reason
to put yourself down!

Use your days to build
yourself up.
You are your own
best cheerleader after all!
Treat yourself like
you would treat a best friend —
with kindness
and compassion
and understanding.
Remember to care about yourself
for who you are,
as you are right now.
That's the most important thing
you could ever do.

GO TEAM!

Ten Great Things
About You

1. You know what's important to you.
2. You have strong values.
3. You've got many amazing ideas and helpful tools in your mind.
4. When you've "fallen," you've always learned something new.
5. You have climbed a mountain... OR twenty-two.
6. You've faced a million different obstacles before.
7. You've gotten over them all.

8. You have courage.
9. You have heart.
10. You don't give up.

You are a shining star,
a bright and remarkable light
forever shooting across
the brilliant and endless sky,
an answer to the dreams
and wishes of someone special,
a rare gem, a beautiful butterfly —
and so much more.

You are you —
one of a kind
and so unique
in every way...
and that's
pretty incredible!

You Have the Power to Get Through Tough Times with a Smile

You can overcome anything that life puts in your path. No matter how tough a situation may seem, you're tougher. The universe will never give you more than you can handle at once. So take heart and don't worry too much about anything.

Even in your most difficult hours, you will uncover strength and courage and the ability to overcome anything you may encounter along the way. You'll also discover hope and starlight and maybe even some bright, happy smiles, too — because they can find a way to shine through even the toughest times.

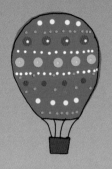

Whatever comes your way, don't ever give up. Have faith, and believe in yourself with all you've got. Remember to have confidence. Trust whatever path you find yourself on — knowing that if you chose it, then it's right for you. Recognize everything you have going for you right now... and keep on being as strong as you can be.

How to Lift Up Your Spirits on a Blue Day

♥ Skim through photographs. You'll see images of people, places, and things that you love, and it will remind you of why you like the world so much.

♥ Watch a movie you've loved for as long as you can remember. Repeat the words to the movie aloud along with the characters. Really get into the plot and lose a piece of yourself there.

♥ Listen to upbeat music. Music gets into your soul, reaches your untapped potential, and reminds you of all you can be. Your feet will be tapping before you know it!

♥ Give yourself the opportunity to laugh. Listen to or watch something you know will give you the giggles, or talk to a friend who can always make you smile. Laugh until your sides hurt and you've got tears streaming down your face.

♥ Read a new book — or an old favorite — from cover to cover, curled up in a special place where you really love to be.

♥ Do whatever it is you were born to do. Only you know how you can make a difference in the world, and you'll feel best when you are doing whatever that is.

Always Look for the Light

In each thing you do,
believe in the courage in you.
Think each day
in a positive way —
"What did I add to life?"
"What did I learn
or teach to others
or myself?"
With each breath,
each step,
each passing year,
what was your takeaway?

See each sunrise as a new start
and every day
as a chance to win.
Above every mountain
you climb,
keep your dreams
in sight...
and always look
for the light.

Every New Day Is a Blank Page

Doing something "yesterday" is the only thing that is impossible today. Today is a blank page — and on it you can write the story of your life. Start from here. Don't fear what you haven't done yet, for you never know until you try. Then try and try again. Learn from the past, but don't get bogged down in it. Create a new narrative, knowing that you can always change it. Each night when you sleep, dream of tomorrow... and the day after that.

The future is a place where
your "always possibles" reside —
and where great things await
as long as you keep
believing in them
...and you.

It Is Up to You!

You are the arbiter
of your own destiny,
maker of your dreams.
You are your own day planner
and night designer.
You are a commander
of your own wings.
You and you alone are the
sole and only one who decides
what will persuade you.
It is up to you to
determine your feelings
and decide what they mean.

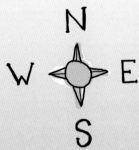

It is up to you to
try to understand
the life you have
and what you can do
to succeed.
It is up to you to follow
your heart and mind and soul
to all the amazing adventures
that are waiting for you.

Give Life
Your Best Shot

Don't talk yourself out of doing the small or giant things. Start talking yourself into doing life's challenging or puzzling activities much more often than you used to. Fear can be the enemy, but don't let it win. Believing a fear to be true can only hinder you in the end — the power's in you.

And though the thought of people judging you might make you blue, do not let it get to you or stop you from aiming high. Give life your very best shot. It's okay if you mess up a time or two... or twenty-two million times. Your tries will still build up. Making an attempt requires bravery. Each time you choose it, you take a step forward — and every time you do that... you're a champion.

The Most Amazing Part of Your Life Is You

Save some room
in your heart
for the impossible.
Worry little, give a lot.
When it comes to
doing the right thing,
do not hesitate.
Carry sunshine
in your pocket.
Aim high.
Don't look too low.
When there's
a storm outside,
do not give in
to grumblings.

Hold a bit
of love inside you
each day.
And whether or not
your star is spinning
up there in the sky...
never forget, in your life,
the most amazing part
is you.

You Are an Amazing Girl

You are powerful and brave.
You are wise and energetic.
You push the envelope
    as far as it can go
    and then some.
You always do your best
    and never make excuses.
You are a great friend
    to those you meet along the way,
    and you serve as a great example
    for others to follow.

You care about your family;
you are giving and understanding
and empathetic.
You always put your whole heart
into whatever you are doing
and never settle for second best.
You never give up,
even when the going is tough,
and you are really there for people
when they need you.
You brighten the lives of others
more than you could ever know.

May You Always Believe in You

May you find rainbows
around every single corner
in your life.
May you wake up
each morning with
a sparkle in your eyes
and sunshine on your face.
May you encounter
peace and love in every way.
May you work hard
and love what you do
with all your heart.

62

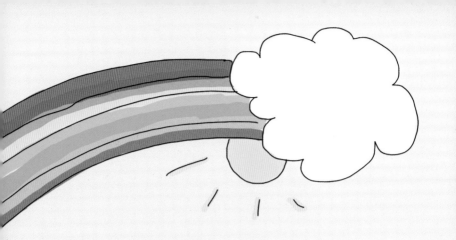

May your hopes soar.
May you be as free as a bird
in the wide-open blue sky.
And most of all,
may you believe
in yourself
every day.

Always believe
in yourself, girl...
because you are meant
for great things!